TRAVEL JOURNAL

DATE: | PLACE:

HOW I FELT TODAY:

WHAT I'VE SEEN TODAY:

_____
_____
_____
_____
_____
_____
_____
_____
_____
_____
_____
_____

WHAT I ATE TODAY:

_____
_____
_____
_____
_____

HOW DID WE TRAVEL:

THE BEST THING THAT HAPPENED TOODAY:

_____
_____

THE WEATHER TODAY WAS:

PLACE FOR DRAWINGS, PAINTINGS, WRITING, ENTRY TICKETS, PICTURES OR ALL THE OTHER STUFF YOU WANT TO CAPTURE

Date: Place:

How I felt Today:

What I've Seen today:

_____
_____
_____
_____
_____
_____
_____
_____
_____
_____

What I Ate Today:

_____
_____
_____
_____

How did we Travel:

The Best Thing that happened tooday:

_____
_____

The Weather today was:

PLACE FOR DRAWINGS, PAINTINGS, WRITING, ENTRY TICKETS, PICTURES OR ALL THE OTHER STUFF YOU WANT TO CAPTURE

Date: Place:

How I felt Today:

What I've Seen today:

_____
_____
_____
_____
_____
_____

_____
_____
_____
_____
_____

What I Ate Today:

_____
_____
_____
_____
_____

How did we Travel:

The Best Thing that happened tooday:
_____
_____

The Weather today was:

PLACE FOR DRAWINGS, PAINTINGS, WRITING, ENTRY TICKETS, PICTURES OR ALL THE OTHER STUFF YOU WANT TO CAPTURE

Date: Place:

How I felt Today:

What I've Seen today:

_____
_____
_____
_____
_____
_____
_____
_____
_____
_____
_____

What I Ate Today:

_____
_____
_____
_____
_____

How did we Travel:

The Best Thing that happened tooday:

_____
_____

The Weather today was:

PLACE FOR DRAWINGS, PAINTINGS, WRITING, ENTRY TICKETS, PICTURES OR ALL THE OTHER STUFF YOU WANT TO CAPTURE

Date: Place:

How I felt Today:

What I've Seen today:	What I Ate Today:
_____	_____
_____	_____
_____	_____
_____	_____
_____	_____
_____	How did we Travel:
_____	
_____	
_____	
_____	
_____	

The Best Thing that happened Tooday:
_____
_____

The Weather today was:

PLACE FOR DRAWINGS, PAINTINGS, WRITING, ENTRY TICKETS, PICTURES OR ALL THE OTHER STUFF YOU WANT TO CAPTURE

Date: _____ Place: _____

How I felt Today:

What I've Seen today:

_____
_____
_____
_____
_____
_____
_____
_____
_____
_____
_____

What I Ate Today:

_____
_____
_____
_____
_____

How did we Travel:

The Best Thing that happened tooday:

_____
_____

The Weather today was:

PLACE FOR DRAWINGS, PAINTINGS, WRITING, ENTRY TICKETS, PICTURES OR ALL THE OTHER STUFF YOU WANT TO CAPTURE

DATE: | PLACE:

HOW I FELT TODAY:

WHAT I'VE SEEN TODAY:
_____
_____
_____
_____
_____
_____
_____
_____
_____
_____
_____

WHAT I ATE TODAY:
_____
_____
_____
_____
_____

HOW DID WE TRAVEL:

THE BEST THING THAT HAPPENED TOODAY:
_____
_____

THE WEATHER TODAY WAS:

PLACE FOR DRAWINGS, PAINTINGS, WRITING, ENTRY TICKETS, PICTURES OR ALL THE OTHER STUFF YOU WANT TO CAPTURE

Date: ⋮ Place:

How I felt Today:

What I've Seen today: ⋮ What I Ate Today:

_____ ⋮ _____
_____ ⋮ _____
_____ ⋮ _____
_____ ⋮ _____
_____ ⋮ _____
_____ ⋮ _____
_____ ⋮ How did we Travel:
_____
_____
_____
_____
_____
_____

The Best Thing that happened tooday:
_____
_____

The Weather today was:

PLACE FOR DRAWINGS, PAINTINGS, WRITING, ENTRY TICKETS, PICTURES OR ALL THE OTHER STUFF YOU WANT TO CAPTURE

Date: Place:

How I felt Today:

What I've Seen today:

_____
_____
_____
_____
_____
_____
_____
_____
_____
_____
_____
_____

What I Ate Today:

_____
_____
_____
_____
_____

How did we Travel:

The Best Thing that happened tooday:

_____
_____

The Weather today was:

PLACE FOR DRAWINGS, PAINTINGS, WRITING, ENTRY TICKETS, PICTURES OR ALL THE OTHER STUFF YOU WANT TO CAPTURE

Date: .... Place: ....

How I felt Today:

What I've Seen today:

_____
_____
_____
_____
_____
_____
_____
_____
_____
_____
_____

What I Ate Today:

_____
_____
_____
_____

How did we Travel:

The Best Thing that happened tooday:

_____
_____

THe Weather today was:

PLACE FOR DRAWINGS, PAINTINGS, WRITING, ENTRY TICKETS, PICTURES OR ALL THE OTHER STUFF YOU WANT TO CAPTURE

Date: .... Place: ....

How I felt Today:

What I've Seen today:

_____
_____
_____
_____
_____
_____
_____
_____
_____
_____
_____

What I Ate Today:

_____
_____
_____
_____

How did we Travel:

The Best Thing that happened tooday:

_____
_____

THe Weather today was:

PLACE FOR DRAWINGS, PAINTINGS, WRITING, ENTRY TICKETS, PICTURES OR ALL THE OTHER STUFF YOU WANT TO CAPTURE

Date: | Place:

How I felt Today:

What I've Seen today:

_____
_____
_____
_____
_____
_____
_____
_____
_____
_____
_____

What I Ate Today:

_____
_____
_____
_____
_____

How did we Travel:

The Best Thing that happened tooday:

_____
_____

The Weather today was:

PLACE FOR DRAWINGS, PAINTINGS, WRITING, ENTRY TICKETS, PICTURES OR ALL THE OTHER STUFF YOU WANT TO CAPTURE

Date: _____ Place: _____

How I felt Today:

What I've Seen today:

_____
_____
_____
_____
_____
_____
_____
_____
_____
_____
_____

What I Ate Today:

_____
_____
_____
_____
_____

How did we Travel:

The Best Thing that happened tooday:

_____
_____

THe Weather today was:

PLACE FOR DRAWINGS, PAINTINGS, WRITING, ENTRY TICKETS, PICTURES OR ALL THE OTHER STUFF YOU WANT TO CAPTURE

Date: Place:

How I felt Today:

What I've Seen today:

_____
_____
_____
_____
_____
_____
_____
_____
_____
_____
_____
_____

What I Ate Today:

_____
_____
_____
_____
_____

How did we Travel:

The Best Thing that happened tooday:

_____
_____

The Weather today was:

PLACE FOR DRAWINGS, PAINTINGS, WRITING, ENTRY TICKETS, PICTURES OR ALL THE OTHER STUFF YOU WANT TO CAPTURE

Date: | Place:

How I felt Today:

What I've Seen today:

_____
_____
_____
_____
_____
_____
_____
_____
_____
_____
_____
_____

What I Ate Today:

_____
_____
_____
_____

How did we Travel:

The Best Thing that happened tooday:

_____
_____

The Weather today was:

PLACE FOR DRAWINGS, PAINTINGS, WRITING, ENTRY TICKETS, PICTURES OR ALL THE OTHER STUFF YOU WANT TO CAPTURE

Date: **Place:**

How I felt Today:

What I've Seen today:

_____

_____

_____

_____

_____

_____

_____

_____

_____

_____

What I Ate Today:

_____

_____

_____

_____

_____

How did we Travel:

The Best Thing that happened tooday:

_____

_____

The Weather today was:

PLACE FOR DRAWINGS, PAINTINGS, WRITING, ENTRY TICKETS, PICTURES OR ALL THE OTHER STUFF YOU WANT TO CAPTURE

Date: | Place:

How I felt Today:

What I've Seen today:

_____
_____
_____
_____
_____
_____
_____
_____
_____
_____
_____
_____

What I Ate Today:

_____
_____
_____
_____

How did we Travel:

The Best Thing that happened tooday:

_____
_____

The Weather today was:

PLACE FOR DRAWINGS, PAINTINGS, WRITING, ENTRY TICKETS, PICTURES OR ALL THE OTHER STUFF YOU WANT TO CAPTURE

Date: _____ | Place: _____

How I felt Today:

😀 😊 😐 😍 😎 😩

What I've Seen today:
_____
_____
_____
_____
_____
_____
_____
_____
_____
_____
_____

What I Ate Today:
_____
_____
_____
_____
_____

How did we Travel:

🚂 ✈️
🚗 🚢

The Best Thing that happened tooday:
_____
_____

The Weather today was:

☀️ ☁️ ⛈️ 🌧️ 🌨️

PLACE FOR DRAWINGS, PAINTINGS, WRITING, ENTRY TICKETS, PICTURES OR ALL THE OTHER STUFF YOU WANT TO CAPTURE

Date: Place:

How I felt Today:

What I've Seen today:

_____
_____
_____
_____
_____
_____
_____
_____
_____
_____
_____
_____

What I Ate Today:

_____
_____
_____
_____
_____

How did we Travel:

The Best Thing that happened tooday:

_____
_____

The Weather today was:

PLACE FOR DRAWINGS, PAINTINGS, WRITING, ENTRY TICKETS, PICTURES OR ALL THE OTHER STUFF YOU WANT TO CAPTURE

DATE: PLACE:

HOW I FELT TODAY:

WHAT I'VE SEEN TODAY:

_____
_____
_____
_____
_____
_____
_____
_____
_____
_____
_____

WHAT I ATE TODAY:

_____
_____
_____
_____
_____

HOW DID WE TRAVEL:

THE BEST THING THAT HAPPENED TOODAY:

_____
_____

THE WEATHER TODAY WAS:

PLACE FOR DRAWINGS, PAINTINGS, WRITING, ENTRY TICKETS, PICTURES OR ALL THE OTHER STUFF YOU WANT TO CAPTURE

Date: _____ Place: _____

How I felt Today:

What I've Seen today:

_____
_____
_____
_____
_____
_____
_____
_____
_____
_____
_____

What I Ate Today:

_____
_____
_____
_____
_____

How did we Travel:

The Best Thing that happened tooday:

_____
_____

The Weather today was:

PLACE FOR DRAWINGS, PAINTINGS, WRITING, ENTRY TICKETS, PICTURES OR ALL THE OTHER STUFF YOU WANT TO CAPTURE

Date: Place:

How I felt Today:

What I've Seen today:

_____
_____
_____
_____
_____
_____
_____
_____
_____
_____
_____

What I Ate Today:

_____
_____
_____
_____

How did we Travel:

The Best Thing that happened tooday:

_____
_____

THe Weather today was:

PLACE FOR DRAWINGS, PAINTINGS, WRITING, ENTRY TICKETS, PICTURES OR ALL THE OTHER STUFF YOU WANT TO CAPTURE

Date: _____ Place: _____

How I felt Today:

What I've Seen today:

_____
_____
_____
_____
_____
_____
_____
_____
_____
_____
_____
_____
_____

What I Ate Today:

_____
_____
_____
_____
_____

How did we Travel:

The Best Thing that happened tooday:

_____
_____

The Weather today was:

PLACE FOR DRAWINGS, PAINTINGS, WRITING, ENTRY TICKETS, PICTURES OR ALL THE OTHER STUFF YOU WANT TO CAPTURE

Date: Place:

How I felt Today:

What I've Seen today:

_____
_____
_____
_____
_____
_____
_____
_____
_____
_____
_____
_____

What I Ate Today:

_____
_____
_____
_____
_____

How did we Travel:

The Best Thing that happened tooday:

_____
_____

The Weather today was:

PLACE FOR DRAWINGS, PAINTINGS, WRITING, ENTRY TICKETS, PICTURES OR ALL THE OTHER STUFF YOU WANT TO CAPTURE

Date: _____ Place: _____

How I felt Today:

😀 🙂 😐 🤩 😎 😩

What I've Seen today:
_____
_____
_____
_____
_____
_____
_____
_____
_____
_____

What I Ate Today:
_____
_____
_____
_____

How did we Travel:

🚂 ✈️
🚗 🚢

The Best Thing that happened tooday:
_____
_____

The Weather today was:

☀️ ☁️ ⛈️ 🌧️ 🌨️

PLACE FOR DRAWINGS, PAINTINGS, WRITING, ENTRY TICKETS, PICTURES OR ALL THE OTHER STUFF YOU WANT TO CAPTURE

Date: Place:

How I felt Today:

What I've Seen today:

_____
_____
_____
_____
_____
_____
_____
_____
_____
_____

What I Ate Today:

_____
_____
_____
_____

How did we Travel:

The Best Thing that happened tooday:

_____
_____

The Weather today was:

PLACE FOR DRAWINGS, PAINTINGS, WRITING, ENTRY TICKETS, PICTURES OR ALL THE OTHER STUFF YOU WANT TO CAPTURE

Date: Place:

How I felt Today:

What I've Seen today:

_____

_____

_____

_____

_____

_____

_____

_____

_____

_____

_____

_____

What I Ate Today:

_____

_____

_____

_____

_____

How did we Travel:

The Best Thing that happened tooday:

_____

_____

The Weather today was:

PLACE FOR DRAWINGS, PAINTINGS, WRITING, ENTRY TICKETS, PICTURES OR ALL THE OTHER STUFF YOU WANT TO CAPTURE

Date: Place:

How I felt Today:

What I've Seen today:

_____
_____
_____
_____
_____
_____
_____
_____
_____
_____
_____
_____

What I Ate Today:

_____
_____
_____
_____

How did we Travel:

The Best Thing that happened tooday:
_____
_____

The Weather today was:

PLACE FOR DRAWINGS, PAINTINGS, WRITING, ENTRY TICKETS, PICTURES OR ALL THE OTHER STUFF YOU WANT TO CAPTURE

DATE: | PLACE:

HOW I FELT TODAY:

WHAT I'VE SEEN TODAY:

_____
_____
_____
_____
_____
_____
_____
_____
_____
_____
_____
_____

WHAT I ATE TODAY:

_____
_____
_____
_____
_____

HOW DID WE TRAVEL:

THE BEST THING THAT HAPPENED TOODAY:

_____
_____

THE WEATHER TODAY WAS:

PLACE FOR DRAWINGS, PAINTINGS, WRITING, ENTRY TICKETS, PICTURES OR ALL THE OTHER STUFF YOU WANT TO CAPTURE

Date: Place:

How I felt Today:

What I've Seen today:

_____
_____
_____
_____
_____
_____
_____
_____
_____
_____
_____

What I Ate Today:

_____
_____
_____
_____
_____

How did we Travel:

The Best Thing that happened tooday:

_____
_____

The Weather today was:

PLACE FOR DRAWINGS, PAINTINGS, WRITING, ENTRY TICKETS, PICTURES OR ALL THE OTHER STUFF YOU WANT TO CAPTURE

Date: | Place:

How I felt Today:

What I've Seen today:

_____
_____
_____
_____
_____
_____
_____
_____
_____
_____
_____
_____
_____

What I Ate Today:

_____
_____
_____
_____
_____

How did we Travel:

The Best Thing that happened tooday:

_____
_____

The Weather today was:

PLACE FOR DRAWINGS, PAINTINGS, WRITING, ENTRY TICKETS, PICTURES OR ALL THE OTHER STUFF YOU WANT TO CAPTURE

DATE: | PLACE:

HOW I FELT TODAY:

WHAT I'VE SEEN TODAY:

_____
_____
_____
_____
_____
_____
_____
_____
_____
_____

WHAT I ATE TODAY:

_____
_____
_____
_____

HOW DID WE TRAVEL:

THE BEST THING THAT HAPPENED TOODAY:

_____
_____

THE WEATHER TODAY WAS:

PLACE FOR DRAWINGS, PAINTINGS, WRITING, ENTRY TICKETS, PICTURES OR ALL THE OTHER STUFF YOU WANT TO CAPTURE

Date: Place:

How I felt Today:

What I've Seen today:

_____
_____
_____
_____
_____
_____
_____
_____
_____
_____
_____

What I Ate Today:

_____
_____
_____
_____
_____

How did we Travel:

The Best Thing that happened tooday:

_____
_____

The Weather today was:

PLACE FOR DRAWINGS, PAINTINGS, WRITING, ENTRY TICKETS, PICTURES OR ALL THE OTHER STUFF YOU WANT TO CAPTURE

Date: | Place:

How I felt Today:

😀 🙂 😐 😍 😎 😩

What I've Seen today:

_____
_____
_____
_____
_____
_____
_____
_____
_____
_____
_____
_____

What I Ate Today:

_____
_____
_____
_____
_____

How did we Travel:

The Best Thing that happened tooday:

_____
_____

The Weather today was:

PLACE FOR DRAWINGS, PAINTINGS, WRITING, ENTRY TICKETS, PICTURES OR ALL THE OTHER STUFF YOU WANT TO CAPTURE

DATE: _____ | PLACE: _____

HOW I FELT TODAY:

😀 🙂 😐 😍 😎 😣

WHAT I'VE SEEN TODAY:

_____
_____
_____
_____
_____
_____
_____
_____
_____
_____
_____
_____

WHAT I ATE TODAY:

_____
_____
_____
_____
_____

HOW DID WE TRAVEL:

THE BEST THING THAT HAPPENED TOODAY:

_____
_____

THE WEATHER TODAY WAS:

PLACE FOR DRAWINGS, PAINTINGS, WRITING, ENTRY TICKETS, PICTURES OR ALL THE OTHER STUFF YOU WANT TO CAPTURE

DATE: _____ PLACE: _____

HOW I FELT TODAY:

WHAT I'VE SEEN TODAY:

_____
_____
_____
_____
_____
_____
_____
_____
_____
_____
_____

WHAT I ATE TODAY:

_____
_____
_____
_____
_____

HOW DID WE TRAVEL:

THE BEST THING THAT HAPPENED TOODAY:

_____
_____

THE WEATHER TODAY WAS:

PLACE FOR DRAWINGS, PAINTINGS, WRITING, ENTRY TICKETS, PICTURES OR ALL THE OTHER STUFF YOU WANT TO CAPTURE

Date: Place:

How I felt Today:

What I've Seen today:

_____
_____
_____
_____
_____
_____
_____
_____
_____
_____
_____
_____

What I Ate Today:

_____
_____
_____
_____
_____

How did we Travel:

The Best Thing that happened tooday:

_____
_____

The Weather today was:

PLACE FOR DRAWINGS, PAINTINGS, WRITING, ENTRY TICKETS, PICTURES OR ALL THE OTHER STUFF YOU WANT TO CAPTURE

Date: Place:

How I felt Today:

What I've Seen today:

_____
_____
_____
_____
_____
_____
_____
_____
_____
_____
_____

What I Ate Today:

_____
_____
_____
_____
_____

How did we Travel:

The Best Thing that happened tooday:

_____
_____

The Weather today was:

PLACE FOR DRAWINGS, PAINTINGS, WRITING, ENTRY TICKETS, PICTURES OR ALL THE OTHER STUFF YOU WANT TO CAPTURE

Date: Place:

How I felt Today:

What I've Seen today:

_____
_____
_____
_____
_____
_____
_____
_____
_____
_____
_____

What I Ate Today:

_____
_____
_____
_____
_____

How did we Travel:

The Best Thing that happened tooday:

_____
_____

The Weather today was:

PLACE FOR DRAWINGS, PAINTINGS, WRITING, ENTRY TICKETS, PICTURES OR ALL THE OTHER STUFF YOU WANT TO CAPTURE

DATE: _____ PLACE: _____

HOW I FELT TODAY:

😀 🙂 😐 😍 😎 😫

WHAT I'VE SEEN TODAY:

_____
_____
_____
_____
_____
_____
_____
_____
_____
_____
_____
_____

WHAT I ATE TODAY:

_____
_____
_____
_____
_____

HOW DID WE TRAVEL:

THE BEST THING THAT HAPPENED TOODAY:

_____
_____

THE WEATHER TODAY WAS:

PLACE FOR DRAWINGS, PAINTINGS, WRITING, ENTRY TICKETS, PICTURES OR ALL THE OTHER STUFF YOU WANT TO CAPTURE

Date: _____ Place: _____

How I felt Today:

What I've Seen today:

_____
_____
_____
_____
_____
_____
_____
_____
_____
_____
_____
_____

What I Ate Today:

_____
_____
_____
_____
_____

How did we Travel:

The Best Thing that happened Tooday:

_____
_____

The Weather today was:

PLACE FOR DRAWINGS, PAINTINGS, WRITING, ENTRY TICKETS, PICTURES OR ALL THE OTHER STUFF YOU WANT TO CAPTURE

Date: _____ Place: _____

How I felt Today:

What I've Seen today:	What I Ate Today:
_____	_____
_____	_____
_____	_____
_____	_____
_____	_____
_____	How did we Travel:
_____	
_____	
_____	
_____	

The Best Thing that happened tooday:
_____
_____

The Weather today was:

PLACE FOR DRAWINGS, PAINTINGS, WRITING, ENTRY TICKETS, PICTURES OR ALL THE OTHER STUFF YOU WANT TO CAPTURE

Date: Place:

How I felt Today:

What I've Seen today:

_____
_____
_____
_____
_____
_____
_____
_____
_____
_____
_____

What I Ate Today:

_____
_____
_____
_____
_____

How did we Travel:

The Best Thing that happened tooday:

_____
_____

The Weather today was:

PLACE FOR DRAWINGS, PAINTINGS, WRITING, ENTRY TICKETS, PICTURES OR ALL THE OTHER STUFF YOU WANT TO CAPTURE

Date: | Place:

How I felt Today:

What I've Seen today:

_____
_____
_____
_____
_____
_____
_____
_____
_____
_____
_____
_____

What I Ate Today:

_____
_____
_____
_____
_____

How did we Travel:

The Best Thing that happened tooday:

_____
_____

The Weather today was:

PLACE FOR DRAWINGS, PAINTINGS, WRITING, ENTRY TICKETS, PICTURES OR ALL THE OTHER STUFF YOU WANT TO CAPTURE

Date: **Place:**

How I felt Today:

What I've Seen today:

_____
_____
_____
_____
_____
_____
_____
_____
_____
_____
_____

What I Ate Today:

_____
_____
_____
_____
_____

How did we Travel:

The Best Thing that happened tooday:

_____
_____

THe Weather today was:

PLACE FOR DRAWINGS, PAINTINGS, WRITING, ENTRY TICKETS, PICTURES OR ALL THE OTHER STUFF YOU WANT TO CAPTURE

Date: _____ | Place: _____

How I felt Today:

What I've Seen today:

_____
_____
_____
_____
_____
_____
_____
_____
_____
_____
_____

What I Ate Today:

_____
_____
_____
_____
_____

How did we Travel:

The Best Thing that happened tooday:

_____
_____

The Weather today was:

PLACE FOR DRAWINGS, PAINTINGS, WRITING, ENTRY TICKETS, PICTURES OR ALL THE OTHER STUFF YOU WANT TO CAPTURE

Date: | Place:

How I felt Today:

What I've Seen today:

_____
_____
_____
_____
_____
_____
_____
_____
_____
_____
_____

What I Ate Today:

_____
_____
_____
_____
_____

How did we Travel:

The Best Thing that happened tooday:

_____
_____

The Weather today was:

PLACE FOR DRAWINGS, PAINTINGS, WRITING, ENTRY TICKETS, PICTURES OR ALL THE OTHER STUFF YOU WANT TO CAPTURE

Date: | Place:

How I felt Today:

😀 🙂 😐 🥰 😎 😩

What I've Seen today:

_____
_____
_____
_____
_____
_____
_____
_____
_____
_____
_____

What I Ate Today:

_____
_____
_____
_____
_____

How did we Travel:

The Best Thing that happened tooday:

_____
_____

The Weather today was:

PLACE FOR DRAWINGS, PAINTINGS, WRITING, ENTRY TICKETS, PICTURES OR ALL THE OTHER STUFF YOU WANT TO CAPTURE

DATE: _____ | PLACE: _____

HOW I FELT TODAY:

WHAT I'VE SEEN TODAY:

_____
_____
_____
_____
_____
_____
_____
_____
_____
_____
_____

WHAT I ATE TODAY:

_____
_____
_____
_____

HOW DID WE TRAVEL:

THE BEST THING THAT HAPPENED TOODAY:

_____
_____

THE WEATHER TODAY WAS:

PLACE FOR DRAWINGS, PAINTINGS, WRITING, ENTRY TICKETS, PICTURES OR ALL THE OTHER STUFF YOU WANT TO CAPTURE

DATE: _____ | PLACE: _____

HOW I FELT TODAY:

😀 🙂 😐 😍 😎 😥

WHAT I'VE SEEN TODAY:

_____
_____
_____
_____
_____
_____
_____
_____
_____
_____
_____
_____

WHAT I ATE TODAY:

_____
_____
_____
_____
_____

HOW DID WE TRAVEL:

THE BEST THING THAT HAPPENED TOODAY:

_____
_____

THE WEATHER TODAY WAS:

PLACE FOR DRAWINGS, PAINTINGS, WRITING, ENTRY TICKETS, PICTURES OR ALL THE OTHER STUFF YOU WANT TO CAPTURE

Date: Place:

How I felt Today:

What I've Seen today: What I Ate Today:

_____   _____
_____   _____
_____   _____
_____   _____
_____   _____
_____
_____   How did we Travel:
_____
_____
_____
_____
_____

The Best Thing that happened tooday:

_____
_____

The Weather today was:

PLACE FOR DRAWINGS, PAINTINGS, WRITING, ENTRY TICKETS, PICTURES OR ALL THE OTHER STUFF YOU WANT TO CAPTURE

DATE: | PLACE:

HOW I FELT TODAY:

WHAT I'VE SEEN TODAY:

_____
_____
_____
_____
_____
_____
_____
_____
_____
_____
_____
_____

WHAT I ATE TODAY:

_____
_____
_____
_____
_____

HOW DID WE TRAVEL:

THE BEST THING THAT HAPPENED TOODAY:

_____
_____

THE WEATHER TODAY WAS:

PLACE FOR DRAWINGS, PAINTINGS, WRITING, ENTRY TICKETS, PICTURES OR ALL THE OTHER STUFF YOU WANT TO CAPTURE

Date: .... Place: ....

How I felt Today:

What I've Seen today:

_____
_____
_____
_____
_____
_____
_____
_____
_____
_____
_____

What I Ate Today:

_____
_____
_____
_____
_____

How did we Travel:

The Best Thing that happened Tooday:

_____
_____

The Weather today was:

PLACE FOR DRAWINGS, PAINTINGS, WRITING, ENTRY TICKETS, PICTURES OR ALL THE OTHER STUFF YOU WANT TO CAPTURE

Date: | Place:

How I felt Today:

What I've Seen today:

_____
_____
_____
_____
_____
_____
_____
_____
_____
_____
_____

What I Ate Today:

_____
_____
_____
_____
_____

How did we Travel:

The Best Thing that happened tooday:

_____
_____

The Weather today was:

PLACE FOR DRAWINGS, PAINTINGS, WRITING, ENTRY TICKETS, PICTURES OR ALL THE OTHER STUFF YOU WANT TO CAPTURE

DATE: _____ | PLACE: _____

HOW I FELT TODAY:

WHAT I'VE SEEN TODAY:

_____
_____
_____
_____
_____
_____
_____
_____
_____
_____
_____
_____

WHAT I ATE TODAY:

_____
_____
_____
_____
_____

HOW DID WE TRAVEL:

THE BEST THING THAT HAPPENED TOODAY:

_____
_____

THE WEATHER TODAY WAS:

PLACE FOR DRAWINGS, PAINTINGS, WRITING, ENTRY TICKETS, PICTURES OR ALL THE OTHER STUFF YOU WANT TO CAPTURE

DATE: | PLACE:

HOW I FELT TODAY:

WHAT I'VE SEEN TODAY:

_____
_____
_____
_____
_____
_____
_____
_____
_____
_____
_____
_____

WHAT I ATE TODAY:

_____
_____
_____
_____
_____

HOW DID WE TRAVEL:

THE BEST THING THAT HAPPENED TOODAY:

_____
_____

THE WEATHER TODAY WAS:

PLACE FOR DRAWINGS, PAINTINGS, WRITING, ENTRY TICKETS, PICTURES OR ALL THE OTHER STUFF YOU WANT TO CAPTURE

DATE: PLACE:

HOW I FELT TODAY:

WHAT I'VE SEEN TODAY:

_____
_____
_____
_____
_____
_____
_____
_____
_____
_____
_____
_____

WHAT I ATE TODAY:

_____
_____
_____
_____
_____

HOW DID WE TRAVEL:

THE BEST THING THAT HAPPENED TOODAY:

_____
_____

THE WEATHER TODAY WAS:

PLACE FOR DRAWINGS, PAINTINGS, WRITING, ENTRY TICKETS, PICTURES OR ALL THE OTHER STUFF YOU WANT TO CAPTURE

DATE: | PLACE:

HOW I FELT TODAY:

WHAT I'VE SEEN TODAY:

_____
_____
_____
_____
_____
_____
_____
_____
_____
_____
_____
_____

WHAT I ATE TODAY:

_____
_____
_____
_____
_____

HOW DID WE TRAVEL:

THE BEST THING THAT HAPPENED TOODAY:

_____
_____

THE WEATHER TODAY WAS:

PLACE FOR DRAWINGS, PAINTINGS, WRITING, ENTRY TICKETS, PICTURES OR ALL THE OTHER STUFF YOU WANT TO CAPTURE

DATE: PLACE:

HOW I FELT TODAY:

WHAT I'VE SEEN TODAY:

_____
_____
_____
_____
_____
_____
_____
_____
_____
_____
_____
_____

WHAT I ATE TODAY:

_____
_____
_____
_____

HOW DID WE TRAVEL:

THE BEST THING THAT HAPPENED TOODAY:

_____
_____

THE WEATHER TODAY WAS:

PLACE FOR DRAWINGS, PAINTINGS, WRITING, ENTRY TICKETS, PICTURES OR ALL THE OTHER STUFF YOU WANT TO CAPTURE

jonathan kuhla
tempelhofer ufer 15
109 63 berlin
mail: jonathankuhla@gmail.com

Made in the USA
Columbia, SC
25 May 2023